Bain-Marie

Melissa E. Jordan

Bain-Marie
©2015, Melissa E. Jordan
ISBN: 9781937806064
Big Wonderful Press, LLC
Brooklyn, NY

Cover Art ©Linda Hill/ www.theredseeds.co.uk
Design by Big Wonderful Press

All Rights Reserved.

Acknowledgments
Thanks to the following journals and magazines in which versions of these poems first appeared:

"Son-Before-Father" *Agave Magazine*:

"Come, Butter, Come" *The Cossack Review*

"Maria Prophetissa at Her Bath," "Posted…" and "LAL, LOL" *Hitherto—The MUIC Literary Journal*

"Mean; to be Mean," "The Minnesota Tip" and "Pet Milk TV" *Off the Coast*

"Hallows" *Otis Nebula*

"or the errant locks of hair of a man standing with the sun behind" *Squawk Back*

"Shem-el-Nessim" *Terrain.org*

"And, Vaster" *Word Riot*

"Enfleurage" and "Sealing the Frost" *YB Poetry*

Contents

Enfleurage	7
Pet Milk TV	11
And, Vaster	12
LAL, LOL	14
Son-Before-Father	16
Maria Prophetissa at Her Bath	17
Shem-el-Nessim	19
Sealing the Frost	21
The Minnesota Tip	22
Hallows	23
Mean; to be Mean	25
Posted: Please Use This Bin for Shredded Dream Journals Only. Thank You – Regional Refuse District #8	27
Come, Butter, Come	28
Bhratri Dwitiya	30
or the errant locks of hair of a man standing with the sun behind	31
Notes	33

For Michael, Phoebe, and Henry

Enfleurage

1.
It's true rendered beef's more efficient,
But I want nothing of the cleaver's streaked vapor.
    Do you see?

In Grasse they splay tuberose between
    tallow-smeared glass;
Suspend the clear panes on wooden racks until each petal is spent.
Then the impregnated fat, the *pomade*, must itself yield—
    delivered of scent, attended by solvents.

No. I used beeswax from her brother's hives
(He drains that farm of chemicals by the year. It's really
    quite something, the vicious filial slap)
and her scratched Pyrex plates.

2.
Funny that as girls she and I spoke of loss so flippantly.
We mourned the discontinued perfume,
    pined over a missed call—
Then wondered at our elders' flinching
    from the grief-drenched words.

Yet the parfumerie's collapse was no small passing.
That's now clear.
Her copper-topped bottle and silk-ruched
    powder box so kindly returned by the ward nurse—
Unexpected grace notes then,
    but now she dwindles with every inhalation, each lift of the lid.
Now the djinni's grown sullen.

3.
Last winter I ordered a fragrance encyclopedia
    for its catalogue of discontinued perfumes.
It's a strange volume—so full of
Churlish denouncements of the modern aldehydes, yet steeped
    in almost girlish longing for
Cast-aside pastes and oils, for scented mouse-skin gloves. It

Dwells in an oddly sensual manner
    on the trade's underbelly—on
Indole—a heady compound lurking
    in tropical flowers and human waste—and the

Brutal fixatives—
Severed, desiccated pouches of musk deer,
Perineal secretions from tortured civets,
Castor sac beaver resin and
Sea-skimmings of whale sick.

But here: The lost scent's blurry blueprint—
Spice, creamy petals, leather, rind, tobacco.
A wartime perfume hazily analyzed:
Top note, heart, base.
No formula, but a trail to follow
    from citrus-charged uncapping to powdery drydown.

Enough to be going on with, I decided.

4.
The curiosities I've trapped in this cabinet!
Wrestled them into melted beeswax and
    sealed them between Pyrex skins—
Each nested pair clenching an olfactory puzzle piece,
Three shelves positing three notes.

I've cut squares of smoky bomber jacket,
Scattered peppercorns, juniper berries, cardamom pods.
Soaked ancient chapbooks in cognac;
Rejected the indolent florals for milky-breathed botanicals:
    honeysuckle stamen and blackberry leaf.
I've sent for orange blossoms and coffee beans,
Ripped angelica's musky roots from the back border—
I even embedded the perfume cap and
    the last precious powder grains.

Some of it took more time, of course—time to
Strip trees of their lichen and dry the spongy heaps
(Oakmoss anchors the lighter chords, then speaks its own
    strangely seasweet story); to
Coax heat-lusting rockrose from New England soil
    for labdanum -- ambergris' dirt-birthed twin—and to
Harvest spicy carnations and clove pinks, to
Track and capture morels, earth clods and all.

5.
Yes, don't bother saying it: one could easily get lost.
A mind could drift from simple unguent to
    waxen totems and hair clippings, could ponder
Squat ushabti messengers dispatched to
    scent out their mistress in the underworld—
But no. Mad science goes only so far in a pie plate.

Instead, here's the domestic alchemy
    of bamboo scoops and miniature scales,
My tins of *pomade*—a philosopher's dozen.
The bain-marie,
    the melt and congeal.

Lapis philosophorum cloaked in three sacred chords.
Mulled top note, earthen base,
    whispered petal heart.

Pet Milk TV

Don't know what to do with food that's just
    for show, the grandmother said.
With that prim wrist snap she's perfected—you remember—
    she tucked the fanned mango between spoon and fork and
Flicked it onto the grass. Mr.

White Coat, he's always
    putting dago fruit on fish, she hissed.
That was the nephew's pharmacist boyfriend, poor soul.
    I hear it's the family way, labeling suitors—the grandmother's brother once
Pegged her own first love Pet Milk TV, for his
    rabid country courtliness.

You swayed beside me on the bench, humpbacked, and lit
    a fresh cigarette with its brother's tail;
Dropped the spent stub in your beer and watched
    it bump against the Styrofoam wall, hissing and
Dimming.....you recall none of this? Somewhere after that

The aunt went still among the picnic squalor,
    her hand drifting girlishly to the table,
Knuckles skimming redwood, fingers slowly opening
    as if to reveal a magician's palmed scarf.
She drew breath, poised above her past.

I was a careful sort of daughter, she began.

And, Vaster

It's all very well, this endless mania for miniature, for finely-wrought prose (two Inches wide) and mahogany peep boxes—ocular Victorian marvels holding a world entire within one tidy cube. And

listen –there's a portrait maker who travels the Métro de Paris with the most cunning oil set nested in his hand. Each day, he daubs a passenger's likeness on the back of his ticket. Just

think of the sailor etching the great kill upon a whale tooth (the very whale). Of schoolgirls stitching furtive initials—their hearts' desire stretched to breaking within the borders of an embroidery hoop. Ah, but I,

I have empires and fortunes, minions and arenas at my disposal -- the rightful mingled heir of Christo and Nero. I have room to show it clear and show it whole. When pockets are deep

and canvases vast, thing becomes frame becomes thing itself. The living teasing the hypokeimenon from the inert, dead illuminating quick's noumenon. I'll cause a

stone courtyard to be built. Then pillaged. No one may visit for twenty-three years. Nothing growing in the tumbled ruins but a lone fern in one dark corner, the overlooked benediction. Next I'll gut a

Georgian estate. The ballroom becomes aching Atlas hefting sheaves of marble—each slab broader than a mead hall gate—and on the highest stack squats one seed-spilling pomegranate. Behind the

drawing room's locked glass door a black mamba wends endlessly through piles of heaped silver moiré. And so it goes, chamber after chamber, vegetable upon steel, the breathing and the breathed. And, vaster, a domed stadium to shield my woven-walled maze. My warp: rebar poles twelve hands high, twelve inches apart. My weft: League-long spirals of archeology by the dozen. Braided electrical wire. A stitched row (two Inches wide) of love notes liberated from the dead letter office. An endless rosary of the thorniest hawthorn branches, another of placating laurel. Ribbons of beeswax. Ropes of carnival beads. Garlands of hand-pulled

cattail paper. A chain made from the horse leads, dog tags, falcon jesses, cat bells of departed familiars. And the meditation path itself, culled from his lost summers—shredded cedar, sunbleached clamshells, pine needles, red sand and crushed pink gravel. With last breath I'll

acquire the Salar de Uyuni. And in the dead center of each dead mile I'll establish one impossible planting, each smaller than a child's wading pool. A miniature bog floated with cloudberries. The daughter of my courtyard fern. A bonsai forest. The ancient

apothecary's rose, blazing fuck you against its frameless, endless mat of salted white. And the last improbable possible: the herbs of Provence, to crest my burial mound.

LAL, LOL

We slunk between steel tables eyeing
   the horseshoe crab blood, creamy blue and set
For skimming in wide-mouthed flasks—our

   field trip tedium dissolved by the
strange fluid, a mermaid's milkshake. I wanted to
   tip one cool bottle to my lips,

   ease the pale delphinium down my throat.
Lab-struck, I could imagine (would take) no other nourishment:
   a schoolgirl vampire craving that sluggish beauty.

Instead I twisted my greedy fingers together,
   listened unslaked to the researcher
Draining the flasks of mystery as

   relentlessly as she
Milked the crabs of their blood. The secret
   is metallic, she said:

Just as mammalian iron reads lurid red
   once blood hits airstream,
So crabbish copper spills forth
   like sugared robins' eggs.

LAL. Chill acronym. Mining of sea-birthed compounds,
   Limulus amoebocyte lysate, to halt the
Fouling of our own biomechatronical nest—our

Vaccines and anodynes,
   mechanical hearts, carbon hands, disposable sight.
We need. Yet somehow (this once) in our needing, we swerve from

    the hardshelled holocaust, the wholesale shredding of
Crop and gizzard. Even now murmuring fishermen
    scoop the long-tailed beasts with clam rakes, inflicting nothing worse than

Intervals between swimming sessions (That strange movement—the stolid
    soldiering on of the tortoise,
Helmeted beneath a manta's bucking glide)—

    and level them into low-tech rowboats,
Ladle their shells with water, drive them in darkness to somber lab techs
    who strap them to bars for draining before
Retuning them safe to sea, safe as houses, safe as milk.

Even so. Just think what a falling off—
    ancient elixir like the breath of coral, like a
Celestial finger set Alice-blue milkglass to rippling—all

Squandered on a species crouched before
    light-leaching screens and concave keys;
Falsely typing mirthful code,
Pressing out our stonefaced oaths—

I am laughing out loud I am rolling on the floor

Son-Before-Father

I hate to tell you, dear, how long I'd lived here before
    I saw that the bright disks
Shouldering aside muddy slush weren't
    early dandelions,
(My toddler hands would have guessed this, would
    have twitched to make dandy chains—
    then, stumbling over strangely tough stalks, would have known
    the ruminant's shock: Wrong plant)   but instead
Coltsfoot, once called son-before-father
    for its trick of
Throwing up blooms first, then
Mouldering away and leaving a blankness
    before
Slapping the eye with massive greenery, fields of horses' hooves.
    The great stutter.
Like my years, decades really, spent amid interiors
    breathing Pinesol instead of pine,
Never guessing my playground could be returned to me,
And my measuring eyes, my knowing fingers.
All this by way of saying dear heart that
I've started coltsfoot syrup for your cough.
    The flowers clutch the thawing hill now like
Neon-button faucets set to drip.
    This morning I set your letter down; I
Levered my knee into the sinking, stinking earth
    and crabbed my way up the bank;
Ripped out clutches
    of the not-dandelions
Turning trickle to gush.
Now the blossoms and stems coil inside jars, freighted with
    with honey to press out
    precious tussin.
They wait on the counter like chunks of archeology, like
    a child's necklace of flowers
Encased in amber.

Maria Prophetissa at Her Bath

Melanosis

My thoughts come darker now—
The black of lamb's blood drying on hyssop tips,
   the chaos of smeared lintels, dawn-discovered.
I suppose my renown will vaporize, or cling
   like a mist to my brothers
(Our exodus triumvirate will not hold, I see. Yet
Weren't we all Jochebed-born?—
   didn't I play watchdog at his first escape?)—even worse, I see
My name bandied by the kitchen gods. My apparatus rattled by clumsy domestics.
And there's something else—my nimble questions, His

Leukosis

   bleached and blistering answer.
Hush, demons. Fall away with this robe.
Here: solve et coagula. My
Gently warming heart and life's stew
   of blood, sinew, marrow
Cradled in a fleshy alembic,
   itself held by mingled waters
(River holds rain, I remind those who seek me. Vital principal whitens vital principal)—
   and my bath of stone containing all, one sturdy
Outer vessel cupping the exquisite

Xanthosis

   tipping point between dissolution and distillation.
Yes. This golden ferment: The gently warmed heart
   and the softening womb, the simmering brain—
We were three such, once, but—Peace. I see that
   out of the third comes the one that shall be fourth.
I must work.
Will the two gums create a true Matrimony? And
   too I conceive of a tribikos, a still with three necks to
Capture essence and cool it in the narrow chambers.
There is much to do before I leave. Surely I must

Iosis

   achieve a stone for water, a well-rock
Revolving lazily as we travel, opening at my touch only.
I see our parched camp suddenly carpeted with purple blooms, see
Streams and red-leaved herbs slithering from
   beneath the dunes,
Swelling the dugs of the women and the cattle and
Bathing, quenching, the two-legged and the four-legged.
…Beat it if you must, brother.
Rage with that sacred staff of yours when I am gone.
Strike it again and again while the thirsting crowd jeers. Then I will relent, and give.

Shem-el-Nessim

Once, though! Slapped awake by the taunting fumes
   of a halved onion held to his nostrils, he rose to
Join the ritual river walk.
He carried their grandmother's reeking *feseekh*, his brothers hefting
   the sulphurous greens, the colored eggs nested in braided bread—
Crowd-flung, they scented out the equinoxal shock rumored
       to have saved a pharaoh's son.

The wind carries it in its belly; its nurse is the earth.

Then the years, the exile—who knows?
Hollowed it into an annual listless picnic,
   drained of brine, bite, vapor.

He told me these things just before Easter,
Traded them at the doorstep for an earlier parting.
When he left, hearth-bound (I'd hissed),
I stalked the yard, surveyed my weapons to hand—
      the spikes and spears of early spring.

She would not think to do this.
I inventoried new shoots of wild lettuce; marveled how the
Egyptian walking onions had stealthily propelled themselves,
   end-over-end, onto the footpath:
Tips birthing bulbs.

I found clownish early shocks of yellow lupin—
   spared, sprouted brothers of last summer's pickled seeds.
(If I brought him the ginger jar of *termis*,
Would the raised lid conjure his uncle's trick:
Hold each briny disk between the front teeth, tongue-nudging
   the sheer outer layer from the meaty bean?)
She would not think to do this.

I paid out my weeks, salting and sun-drying raw mullet,
   risking botulism from dubiously-translated recipes,
Moving in an amniotic scrum
   of vinegar, liquamen, olive oil, green sap.
I gentled eggshells into soapy water;
Dyed each halved pair in successive baths
   of beet, onion skin, turmeric.   He
   returned.

At first breeze, I pulled the greens, retrieved the salted fish,
Eased the skin off each lupin bean, each one.
I chopped and mixed my harvest, foreign and domestic,
Spooned pungent mounds into marbled shells,
    packed a river map.
Muttered, invoked: the fish, the lettuce, the green onion, the lupin, the egg:
    feseekh, lettuce, onion, *termis*, egg….

Kettle, whisk, mustard powder.
I carried the basin to him, the day's first ritual.
Shem-el-Nessim, I whispered. Smell the breezes.

Sealing the Frost

Come with me. Come with me please, and stop pulling that face. This is how
quests *are*.
        Don't you think this cord rasps my own shoulder, and see how
maddeningly the
                trowel and wooden
stick lurch
            and beat against the sides of my pail?
                        Supplication—
So what that our only crops
            are the pots of strawberry popcorn
      propped outside the cellar door
                        hiding
        our rusted gutters
                and pockmarked vinyl.
Not exactly the terraced fields of Santa Eulalia back here. I know that.
        And not much to protect I suppose
    except
        your vague vision of
            jarred baby ears rubbing lurid
elbows with the paperbacks in your office. Still.
            Climb. Near the top there's that gulley never dry this time
of year, and the two-trunked red oak.
That's where we'll mix the cement and slither bungeed figure-8s
            around the tree's crotch
    and my own: Wood tethering flesh.
           The oak juts over
The line etching the scarred ridge like a primmed-up mouth—that's
                where the frost spirit lives.
        Ease me down with the cement and trowel. I'll do some
    frosting of my own—the
Task's end, smear-swirl meditation
        sacred   to all bakers.
Perhaps a whispered prayer to Ix Chel –
    that's my business.
Listen, it's either all this or you delete her texts and pour the vodka down the sink.

The Minnesota Tip

Her grandfather dug a dozen graves by the time we left for the bus stop
    and the aunts burned the skins of three mice.
In the keeping room a pail of slugs and red sage leaves were fermenting,
  started the night
Moon entered
Cancer.

That was business.
     It was nothing to do with
  hallowtide, with the
Long skirts and the orange cookies we carried in D&L bags,
   wiry handles
Cutting our
  palms. Our ankles reared and bucked
On the rutted hill road.

The mouse ash, I meant to say,
   and the slug slurry were for scaring
pest foragers from the fall crops—
    farmerspeak for behold your foolish brothers, beware
Medieval stakes, impaled heads. Then too
    her grandfather swore by the old Minnesota Tip practice

    for guarding the rosebushes lining his farmstand lot.
He swathed his roses in burlap shrouds
   against frost heaves and
Winterkill. Then he made

a trench for each of the twelve—
   loosened all but a few perimeter roots.
(In those fragile moments the shrubs pivoted
   meekly upright like
Baby teeth clinging to gums)

And he eased his wraiths into their cryogenic pens;
     he covered them with soil and straw.

Hallows

        only that school was a fever dream—black frosting, bells
sounding out of turn,
High shrieks quickly muffled.
Skirt over jeans. Blue eyelids. Charged air and ten minute thunderstorm,
   ozone and ginger,
Tsunami of leaves flung against the cafeteria window.

Then we were wedged in the wheel well of her brother's
   pickup, finished with
Doorbells
   and sweet looting, the
Black streets still wet enough to hurl back
   skimming stars, shards of moon.
Maddie and Eugene were up front with him, I remember.
We passed
   her father's experimental fields,
Slick with

   governmental insecticide.
She switched her skirt to the side
   like tossing a settled cat from her lap and
Staggered up against the racketing slipstream.
C'mon, she yelled and pulled me up

   —gypsies tonight.
Then, who knows why, we kept screaming it.
   Come on! Come on!
Hurling the curse, the benediction, against water towers, service roads,
      the cider mill, the subdivision where my mother cleaned. I'm going

   the orchard path she said when
They dropped us at the shoulder. Less steep.
Last weekend we'd helped hang weights on the
   young pears and we heard them now,

    copper striking copper. I set
My eyes on her surefooted paisley
    progress, but when she turned her eyes were
Open sockets, just awful, and the
    wind wouldn't stop.

Don't think about it just walk through it she called but
I was already rooted, trapped inside
    the gnarled shadows and hammer blows.

She came back for me.
She set her thumbs at my waist,
    evened my lopsided sweater, began
Buttoning it, bottom to top. We were
    holding our breaths. A key was turning. Then she
Led me up away from the dark clanging trees.

Mean; to be Mean

Think about Mercurochrome
         after berrying;
                        or your stickpin
                  jutting like a dislocated joint to cover
         the stain. Downtable

                  his wrist pivots lazily on the neighboring chairback,
         pinning the woman's spread, splayed jacket.
Yes his fingers
            hover above her collar's inner velvet—
         his trademark charged inch, frisson

   of raunch. And to think I was there at the first meal, he says. A
Lovely roast it was. Just imagine
                        (his short British bark)
I witnessed that almighty rock around which our future meals would
      cluster and form:
Planet Casserole
         ruled by my wife, goddess of thrift.

Once his harsh yip served you—
   its brief, blunted gallantry. At the wedding
His cousin rose and ensured
   the two of you a prosp, a preposterous, prosperous! Oh God sorry!
future.
Eye-cuts and half-hearted jeers, Have another, David!—But still the phantom

   images—the green card, the babyfood jars—
Floated cartoonishly above their donnish sculls.
You felt yourself taking on that pinched, sullen look
   women get in their middle months.

But your groom laughed like a gunshot, jutted his chin at
   dinner trays coming from the kitchen (Hey!) and the
Moment passed from chill prophesy to tipsy folly.

Use it up   wear it out   make it do   or do without
                              he's chanting now.
   Never
Call her a drudge, he solemnly
Warns his neighbor.
   It's not parsimony
Oh dear no I am given to hear it's taking life by
The throat. Right, darling?
   she wrings the very heart the pure essence from every last thing

(Marrow, you think—
   how lovely to think of all things marrow now.
Life's juice, one last gift from the bones—
   a stewpot benediction.
   Or remember Poirot reverently setting plump, prized squash on the garden wall.)

Every goddamn thing that grows or moves, he says. Just don't
   say cheap. Old words are
Best words   like preserving,   or close, or   What's the word I want darling?

Posted: Please Use This Bin for Shredded Dream Journals Only. Thank You – Regional Refuse District #8

(A) 4:17 a.m. Monday and Gerald gone three weeks
…After that [illegible] tunneled rooms like Digory Kir{illegible}….first attic the usual overflow of cabbage rose cushions and peach lampshades but [illegible]… into the vivisectionist's annex -- shelves of pickled sparrows and copper scales. I passed into a storehouse of stacked canvases, then a blue-green room filled with watery light. A figure crouched at a kneewall window like a scullery maid before the hearth. I paused, [illegible]whispered hoarsely, "He is behind you. You must run." I reached my o [illegible] yet receding with each step as I descended into my den, knowing I would soon wa[illegible] …cats claiming squatters' rights on the armrests and I breathed with the rhythm of waking and of the pulsing answering ma[illegible] then two noises came. The creaking attic door I'd forgotten to lock, and the unspooling message. "I am coming."

(B) April 25, 193[?]
The old men sitting in the sun.
Count them all, one by one.
All clench portraits of righteousness,
This one's wife in her wedding dress.

(C) [Date unknown] The harvest comes, but we children
 are free to wander among the three sisters,
  Weaving cornsilk wreaths and rattling dried beans
           inside their papery casings.
    Then the sky darkens and spears of wind cut our skin.
  We dive to the precious inches of still air above the   ground;
         elbow aside the prickly squash vines.
    We settle into the still-baking earth
  until our chilled bellies and our scrabbling fingers are warmed,
until
   the sun bleeds through
to cup our skulls,
    Run a beneficent beam along
     each spine.

Come, Butter, Come

Goldenrod smells of sauerkraut when boiled. Its seeds
        roil up in the kettle like caraway. Some always
                escape the strainer; then
Wink in and out of view during kneading. The flower dye

Seeps
        butter yellow
into salt dough,
        Perfect to edge churn-shaped platters,
to frame the stenciled pioneer chant—
        a charm devised
they say
        against the tedium of churning
Peter stands at the gate
Waiting for his buttered cake.
Come, butter, come

Last night I was onto something new, was
Shaping a maiden for the Greensleeves bowl—
        she was to lurk like a hidden life
                on the bottom of the high-sided vessel. And
I was carving the ballad around the rim.

The oven was heating. I'd contrived
Thinly-rolled sheets
        to drape over her pale form—
Marbled dough dyed black walnut and nettle for her bodice
        and a skirt of royal purple stained with elderberries, under a
Silvery green apron tinted with woodruff and alum, and a bundle of
        marigold-washed strands for her hair.
And I was affixing her to the bottom of the bowl
        to squelch and settle into place.

And I did lick my fingers to moisten the raw dough;
And I did marry her skirts, her lissome back, to the bottom of the bowl.

Can we talk about these supplies, he said.
He backhanded the air, a gesture to encompass
        the carving tools, the pigments and scaffolding wire.
                The voice tentative, *Until you're working again*
But it was as if his fingernails scraped away one last filmy scrim.

Then it was that
        The shabbiness of my vision, the outright goddamn cornpone
                of coaxing flour and salt to speak cloth and clay and
    wood—
The shortcuts in my research—
        the cheap fumes of the hardware store varnish—all
Rose up in my throat.

In the pantry the finished bowls and platters were curing.
I seized them all, hurled them past his protests
        to perish on sensible linoleum.
I turned off the oven; pitched the colored doughs into the bin.

I could not bear to mangle my last figure, though. My raw maiden.

Bhratri Dwitiya

Bhratri Dwitiya is "Brothers' Day" and takes place after the new moon of Diwali. Sisters rub the foreheads of their brothers with sandalwood powder and chant good wishes: With this, I forestall the entry of Yama, the god of death, into your life.
  -- Swasti Mitter, Hindu Festivals

The stars are dimmer now,
skinning off the walls and leaking fluorescence with each birthday.
Just as on that night I kissed her soft as new life,
fifteen years on I graze the same cherished temple
(Children, like tennis rackets, have their own sweet spots. Hers
was always a lips' brush between lash and hairline;
His invited sturdier smacks on the reliable crown),
again steal moments against hospital urgency.
I didn't wake her, then—only lingered above
Her last midnight as the beloved only.
Now I shatter sleep with
keep this phone
and *he won't say how many.*
Morning coming, then, meant we could lift her to the plexiglass crib for
her toddler benediction; to
Tap spatulate fingers against his forehead.
This dawn, this now, she eyes the heart monitor;
Passes a suddenly ladylike palm over his swimmer's buzzcut,
across his brow.

or the errant locks of hair of a man standing with the sun behind

Swim against it—fins, teeth, scent—
Pace volcanic black.
Seek the rumored mailbox in
the furthest mangrove stand.
Nudge aside tortoises lumbering giantly;
Take up the tea-colored scroll, the
feathered pen.
Etch a message to all buccaneers
in your wake.

*Brick post office: Sending
your due to those who
know all too well of your
of your whereabouts.*

Stay in keeps of Connemaran cast.
Wring stories from each innkeeper
until final ember and staircase climb.
Keep close the pewter chamberstick.
Trace shapes moving in human,
inhuman form against stone walls.
Gallop to land's end at first light,
Scan the sea breaking, cliffside fathoms
below.

*Tollbooth: Braked against
a single steel arm,
squinting at ghostly
changemakers behind
fly-specked windows.*

Drive him down a blue highway,
giddy on hunger and moonlight.
Abandon asphalt for dirt
and the copper-topped roadhouse.
Drink beer to sting your throats,
Shatter chicken between your thumbs.
Spot the new road from a
single gingham window.
Remember his hands on the wheel.

*Blacktop lot: Your only
companion the red and
white bucket, spotted and
spreading with grease.*

Trod the soft ground of bluegrass heaven,   *Auto-shop counter:*
borne by seven fiddles.   *Hearing, as if through a*
Dent your cheek on the   *pinhole, a distant radio.*
shirtfront rivets of strangers,
Suspend your sandals
from the tip of one finger;
Let go.

Peddle red sandstone lanes in maritime.   *Chin in hand you watch,*
Follow the wood-silver tunnel to a   *with perfect*
sea trail turning, beech unto beach.   *concentration, the*
Fling self and bike down forbidden dunes;   *drag-dance of crabs.*
Stretch across a blood orange slab cantilevering
the cove.

Notes

p. 4
The Pet Milk Show, sometimes called Pet Milk TV, was televised from the Grand Ole Opry in the 1950s and '60s. Artists like Patsy Cline, Stringbean and Grandpa Jones appeared on the broadcasts.

p. 9
Maria Prophetissa was an Egyptian alchemist believed to have lived during the first century B.C. She is credited with inventing a number of scientific apparatus, including the tribikos and the bain-marie (one of the few ways in which her name lives on). She also developed a GrecoEgyptian system of explaining chemical reactions by listing their four colors or mystical stages: Melanosis /Black (chaos), Leukosis/White (cleansing), Xanthosis/Yellow (ferment), and Iosis/ Red or Purple (culmination).
In legend, Maria is also Miriam, the sister of Moses and Aaron. Miriam's place in Jewish, Christian and Islamic texts is elusive. Along with her brothers, she was one of the three crucial prophets of the Exodus, yet God struck only her with a skin-whitening rash after she and Aaron questioned one of His proclamations. During the desert odyssey, Miriam provided water for the followers through her miraculous well-rock. After her death, Moses was chastised by God for striking it more than once, having lost faith in its power to deliver.
Author Mark Haeffner observes that while there is no conclusive proof that Maria and Miriam were one in the same, Maria "seems to have embraced both aspects of the tradition: the mystical, prophetic, gnomist approach as well as the strictly practical laboratory, experimental aspect."

p. 11
"A national holiday and folk festival in Egypt, the Shem-el-Nessim has been observed for thousands of years as a day to smell the breezes and celebrate spring. Nessim means 'zephyr,' the spring breeze, and shem means 'to breathe in.' Traditionally, people pack picnics to have outings along the Nile River or in parks. Certain food is specified for the occasion: the main dish is fessikh, a kind of salted fish."
-- Holidays, Festivals, and Celebrations of the World

p.13
"The Cuchumatan Indians of Santa Eulalia in northern Guatemala hold a rather risky ceremony [known as Sealing the Frost] every year early in the planting season. The town of Santa Eulalia is perched high in the mountains and the Indians traditionally believe that the cold frost resides in a crack over the edge of a cliff outside town. In order to protect the new crops from a late frost, the religious leaders in town lead a procession to the cliff. They tie a rope around the waist of one of the leaders and lower him over the edge where he fills in the crack with cement to keep the frost in."
-- Holidays, Festivals, and Celebrations of the World

p.14
"The wave front is as it were bisected by the body and the traces of this injury result in blurring of the margin of the shadow.... Fine blades of grass and spiders' webs on the crest of a hill with the sun behind it, or the errant locks of hair of a man standing with the sun behind, often light up mysteriously by diffracted light, and the visibility of smoke and mist is based on it."
-- Erwin Schrödinger, The Fundamental Idea of Wave Mechanics

www.ingramcontent.com/pod-product-compliance
Lightning Source LLC
Chambersburg PA
CBHW021455080526
44588CB00009B/857